Helping Hands

Written by Frances Bacon
Photography by Wayne Barrett

Costa Rica

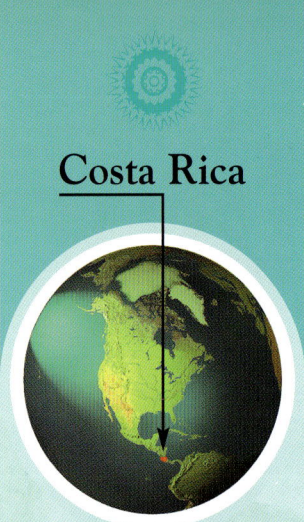

Laura travels from her home in Canada to the rainforests of Costa Rica to go on assignment with her photographer dad. She visits a sloth sanctuary called Aviarios del Caribe and learns firsthand about the importance of kindness when caring for orphaned animals.

kindness helping others

Costa Rica

Laura visits a sloth sanctuary in Costa Rica. She learns the importance of kindness while taking care of Buttercup and Rosebud, two orphaned sloths. She also learns how sloths live in the wild.

COSTA RICA COLLECTION

ISBN 978-0-7406-3490-1

ETA 403161

Titles in Set D

Other Country Collections in the Series

Set E
- Canada
- Italy
- Mexico
- Peru
- Russia
- U.S.A.
- West Africa

Set F
- Caribbean
- Ireland
- Japan
- Mexico
- Nepal
- U.S.A.
- Vietnam

Set G
- Brazil
- Cambodia
- Egypt
- France
- Scotland
- Turkey
- U.S.A.

What Do You Think?

1. What would Laura have learned from her trip to Costa Rica?

2. Ecotourism is important to Costa Rica. How can we show respect and responsibility toward the place where we live?

> Why would kindness be important for a person who works in an animal sanctuary?

Index

coffee	22
ecotourists	18–19
endangered animals	16–18
national parks	16–17
oxcarts	22
predators	10
rainforests	13, 16, 18–21
sanctuaries	5–6, 8–9, 12
San José	15, 23
satellite transmitters	11
sloths	5–6, 8–13

Performing Arts

Artists from around the world perform at the National Theater (above) in San José. Some of the theater's statues were made by Italian artists many years ago and shipped to Costa Rica.

Showtime!

Costa Rica has a long history of the arts. Its National Theater is more than 100 years old. It was built when an Italian opera singer was invited to sing in Costa Rica. He refused to come unless a theater was built for him. Some people in the coffee business donated the money for the theater to be built.

Costa Rica is famous for its coffee. Long ago, oxcarts were used to transport coffee beans from the fields to the ports. Costa Rican oxcarts are an important art form. They are painted red and then beautifully decorated by hand. Once a year, they appear in a colorful parade.

Today, children from all around the world raise funds and donate money to help save rainforests. The money helps buy more land and goes toward education and scientific research.

Children's Rainforest

There is a special rainforest in Costa Rica. It is called the Children's Eternal Rainforest. In 1987, some Swedish children were learning about rainforests. They wanted to help save a rainforest from destruction in Costa Rica. They had a bake sale and sold paintings, cards, and crafts. The money helped preserve the rainforest.

What other kinds of things can children do to help their environment and the animals and plants that live in it?

destruction   the action of destroying something

Canopy tours go into the upper level of a rainforest. Tourists can ride in a cable car or walk on bridges through the treetops. Some tours even let people slide between platforms on special sliding equipment.

Ecotourists

Ecotourists flock to Costa Rica every year. These are tourists who like to view plants, animals, and the natural environment firsthand. The idea of ecotourism first came from Costa Rica.

Ecotourists can watch endangered turtles hatch and run into the ocean. They can visit butterfly gardens. They can even walk in the canopy of a rainforest!

Monteverde Butterfly Farm

canopy   the top layer of trees in a forest

The money that tourists pay to enter the national parks goes toward protecting these special environments.

In Need of Help

Jaguar

Green sea turtle

Manatee

Howler monkey

Giant anteaters

Are any animals in your country endangered? What is being done to help them?

National Parks

Costa Rica is famous for its national park system. Beaches, rainforests, coral reefs, volcanoes, and caves can be found throughout Costa Rica. There are hundreds of different kinds of animals and plants living in the national parks, too. Some of them are endangered. Today, people are helping to save these animals and plants.

endangered   close to becoming one of the last left on Earth

Costa Rica's capital is San José. It is a busy city with modern buildings and an international airport.

On the Go!

What is an ecotourist?
Go to page 18

Why did some Swedish children raise money for a rainforest in Costa Rica?
Go to page 20

What were oxcarts first used for in Costa Rica?
Go to page 22

 # Explore Costa Rica

Long ago, Spanish explorers named the country of Costa Rica. The name means "rich coast." The explorers believed that the country had rich resources of gold and other metals. They soon found that Costa Rica's best resources were good soil and plenty of rain. Costa Rica has a tropical climate with both a rainy season and a dry season.

People in Costa Rica are proud of their country. They protect and care for their beautiful environment.

resource something from nature that is available for people to use

Did You Know?

Sloths spend nearly all of their lives upside down in trees. They even sleep upside down! They use their strong claws to hang onto branches.

Sloths eat leaves, buds, and young twigs. In the wild, they live only in the rainforests of Central and South America.

Laura felt sad saying goodbye to her new friends, but she also felt happy. She knew that Buttercup and Rosebud would be safe and well protected at the sloth sanctuary in Costa Rica.

Lost and Found

Tracking instruments, such as satellite transmitters, are very useful to scientists. They let scientists find and monitor groups of animals, animals on the move, and even animals that have been released into the wild after being in captivity.

There can be problems with tracking transmitters though. Sometimes they fall off the animals. The batteries can also run out!

Trina and Laura used a tracking instrument to help them find a sloth named Junior. He wears a special radio collar.

Why would being able to track animals be helpful to scientists?

satellite transmitter a device that sends out signals that can be tracked

Sloths move very slowly, but they still can be hard to find. They often have green algae growing on their fur. This helps sloths hide from predators.

predator   an animal that hunts and eats another animal

Trina is a volunteer at the sloth sanctuary. She showed Laura how to hold baby Rosebud.

Trina also taught Laura how to feed tasty treats to Buttercup.

Today, a number of sloths live at the sanctuary. They are cared for by a team of staff and volunteers.

What organizations around the world use volunteers?

volunteer   a person who does a job without being paid

Buttercup came to live with Judy and Luis in 1989. She was very small and very hungry. Judy mixed special milk for Buttercup and fed her with a bottle. Soon, Buttercup became strong and healthy again.

Judy and Luis did such a good job taking care of Buttercup that people started to bring other orphaned sloths to them. So Judy and Luis turned their land into a sanctuary for sloths.

Recently, Laura's dad took her to Costa Rica to meet Buttercup. Buttercup is a three-toed sloth. She lost her mother when she was very young. Now Buttercup lives with Judy and Luis Arroyo at the Aviarios del Caribe sloth sanctuary.

sanctuary   a place where injured or unwanted animals are cared for

Helping Hands

Laura lives in Canada. Her dad is a wildlife photographer. He travels around the world and meets a lot of interesting people. He meets even more interesting animals!

Contents

Helping Hands	4
Explore Costa Rica	14
National Parks	16
Ecotourists	18
Children's Rainforest	20
Showtime!	22
What Do You Think?	24
Index	24